# FISH & GAME

## HUMOR

### By
### Charles Hellman and Robert Tiritilli

35271 Monarch Way
Palm Desert, CA 92211
www.LuckySportsHumor.com

ISBN 0-935938-55-5
Illustrations by Robert A.Tiritilli
Cover & Interior Design by Charles S. Hellman
Edited by Charles S. Hellman

**"I think he's a KEEPER!"**

"Eat your heart out... Charlie Tuna!"

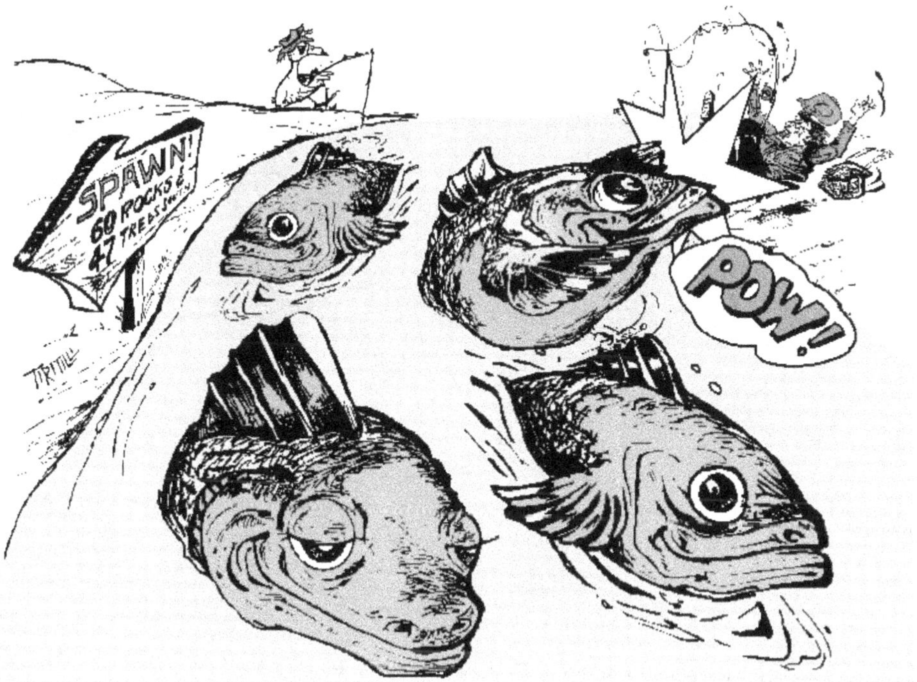
SPAWN!
60 ROCKS &
47 TREES
POW!
TIRITILLI

**"Watch who you're calling HORNY"**

**"He tasted like chicken!"**

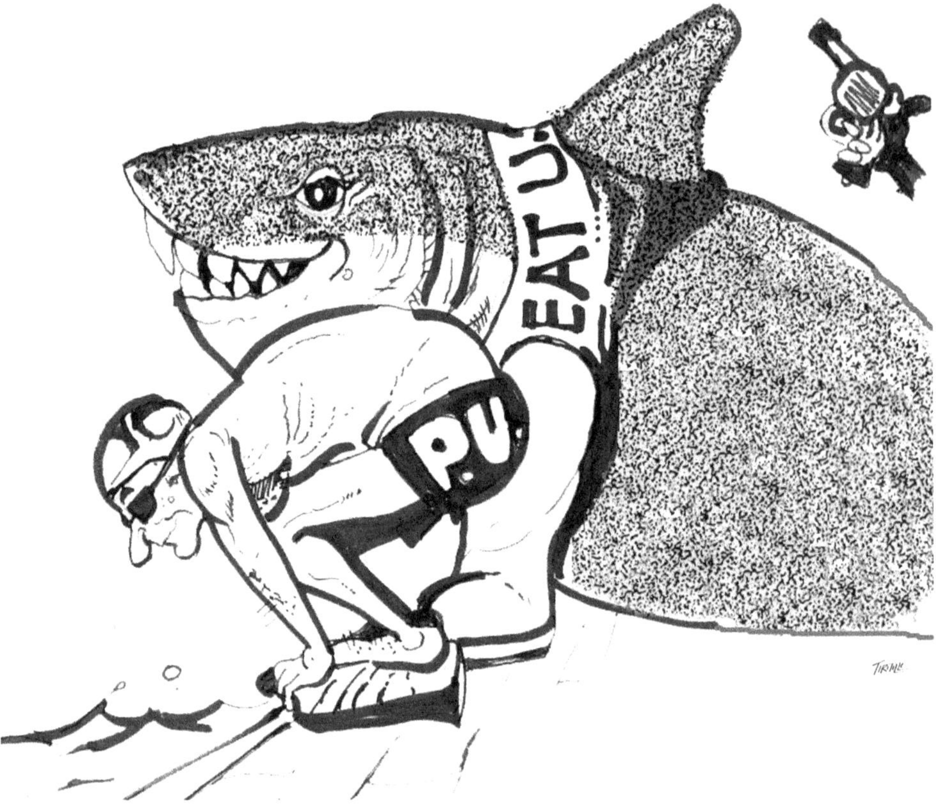
EAT U
P.U.

**Last Race?**

# Two Liars

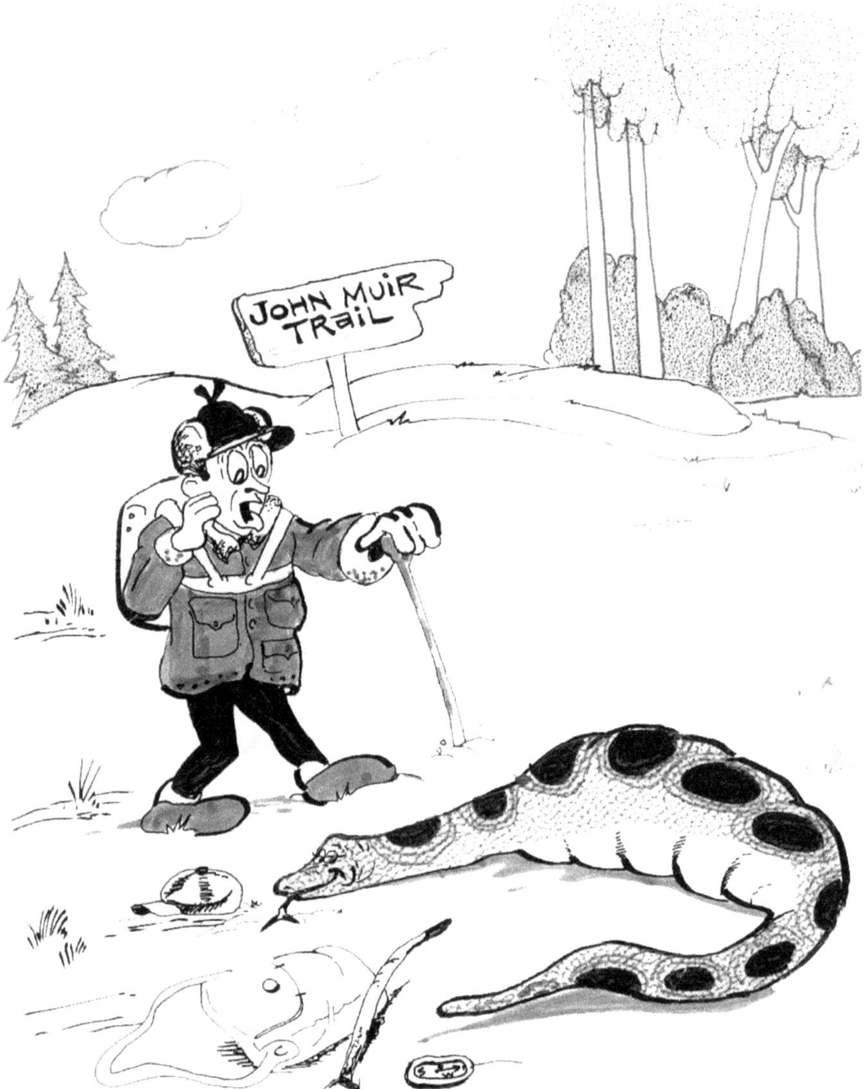
JOHN MUIR
TRAIL

**Wrong Trail**

"Look what he did to my favorite rifle!"

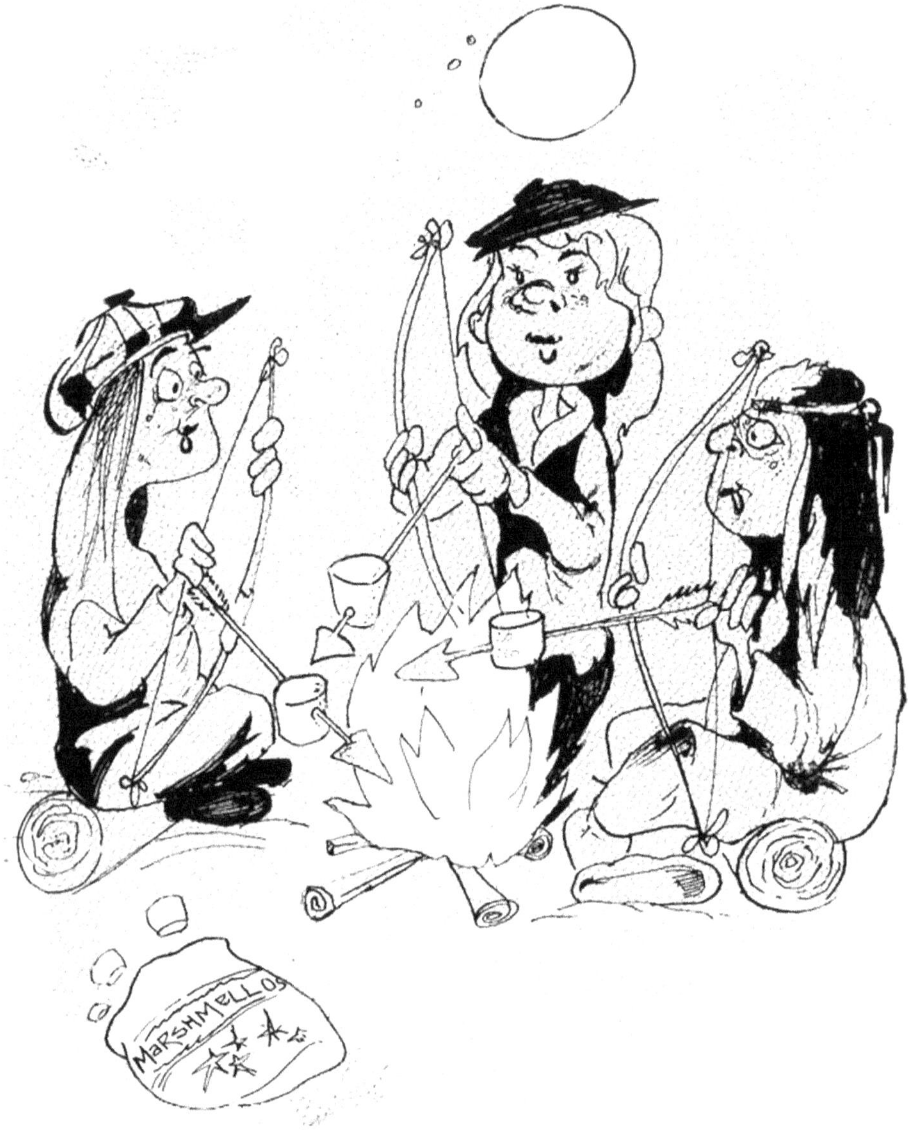
MARSHMELLOS

S'Mores

"See if there's any HONEY."

"I don't think we're SAFE here!"

**Sitting Ducks**

**Trapped**

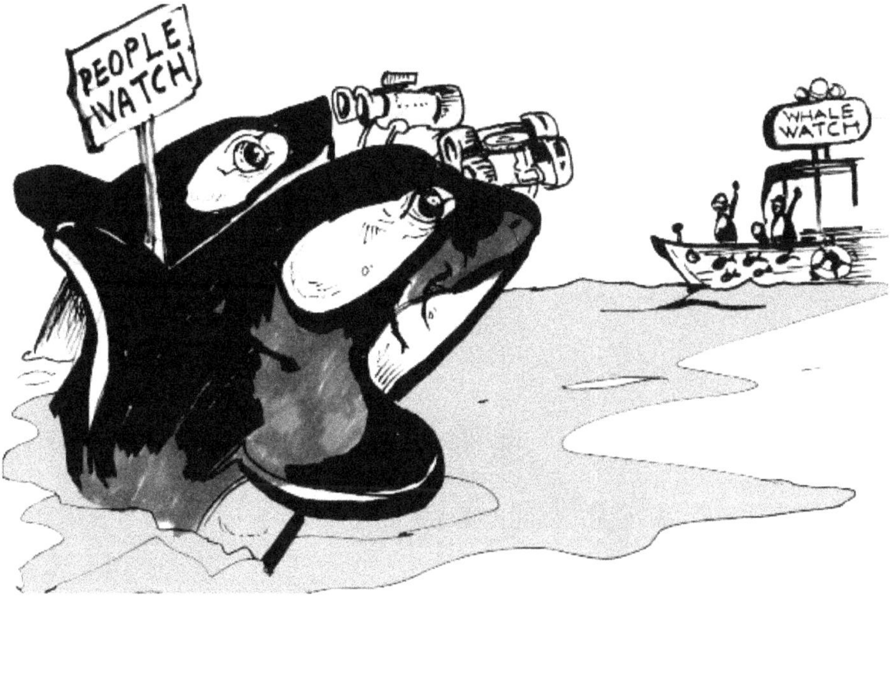
PEOPLE
WATCH
WHALE
WATCH

**I-to-Eye Contact**

**A Little Run Before Dinner!**

TIRTILLI

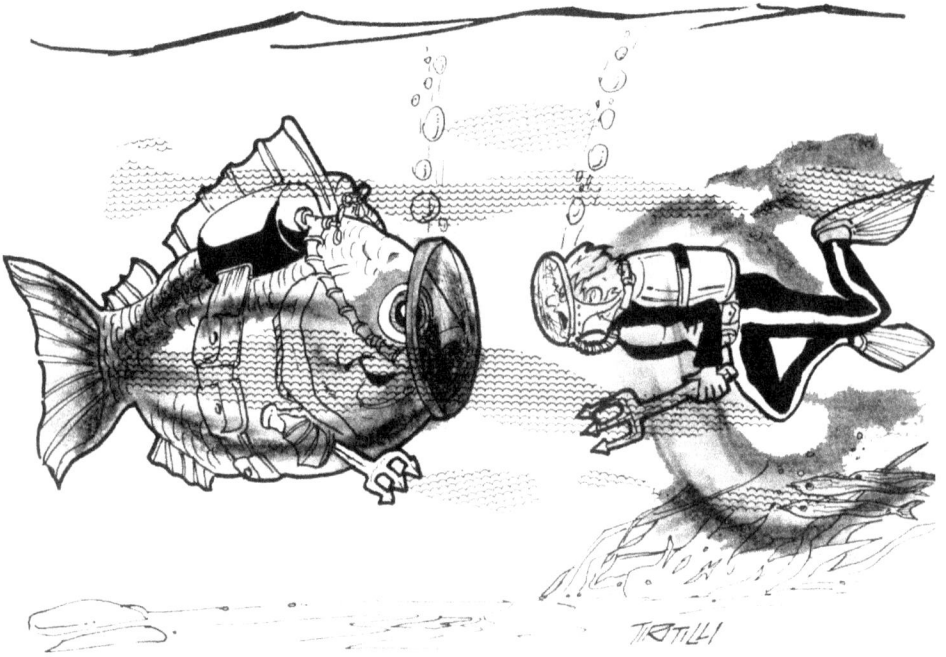

**"Who do you LOVE?"**

BANG! "I got him!"

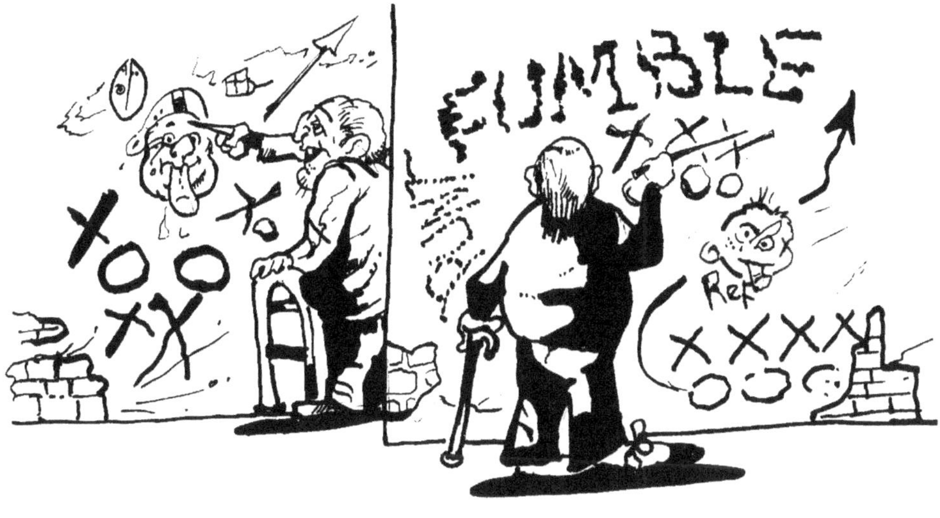
FUMBLE
Rex

"What a bunch of BULL!"

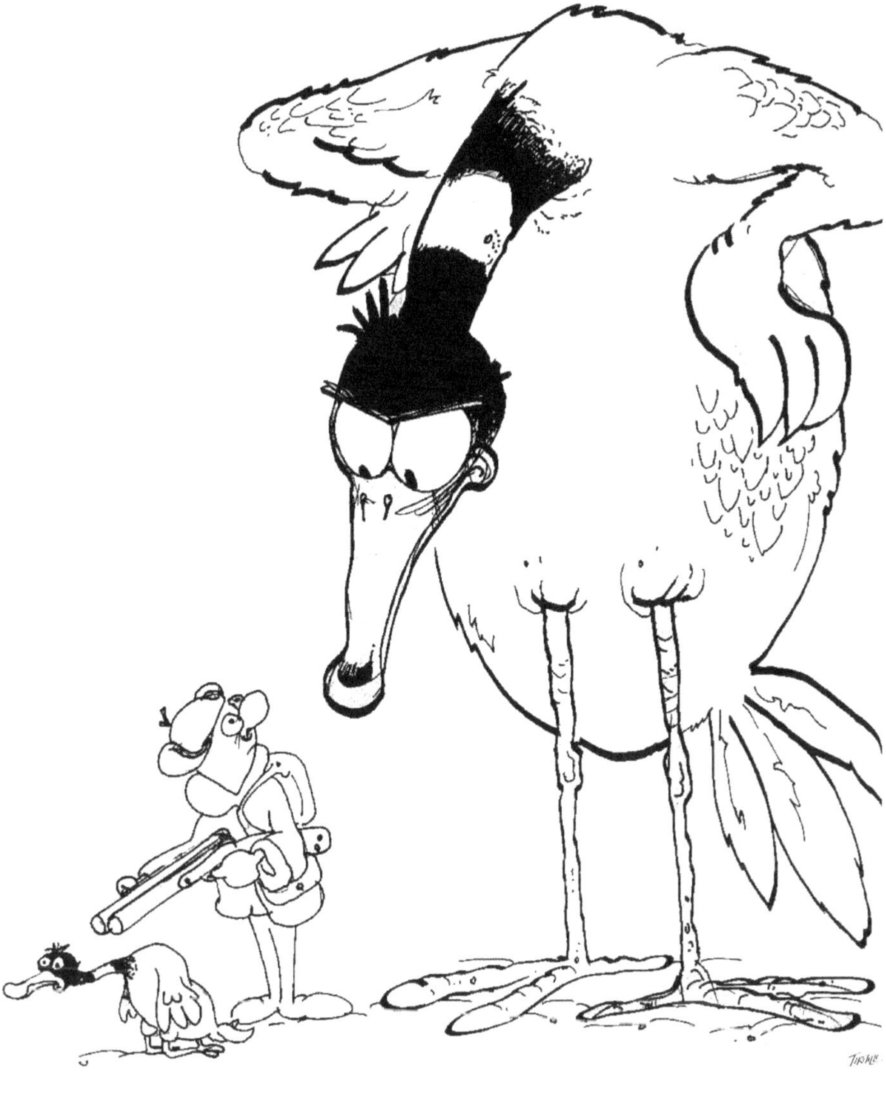

**"Are we on SAFARI or RECRUITING?"**

**Early Sporting Goods Store**

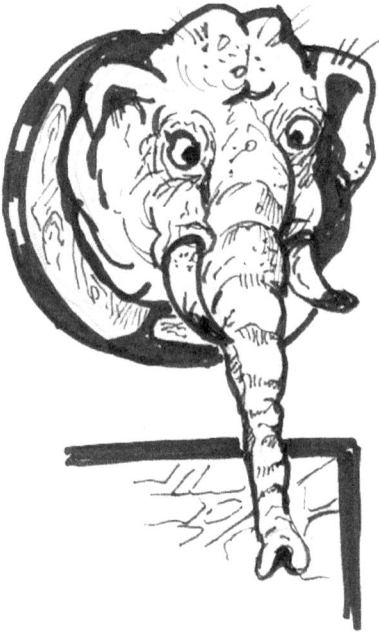

**"Oh, No! Where's My
Mother's Portrait?"**

**Partying before the KILL**

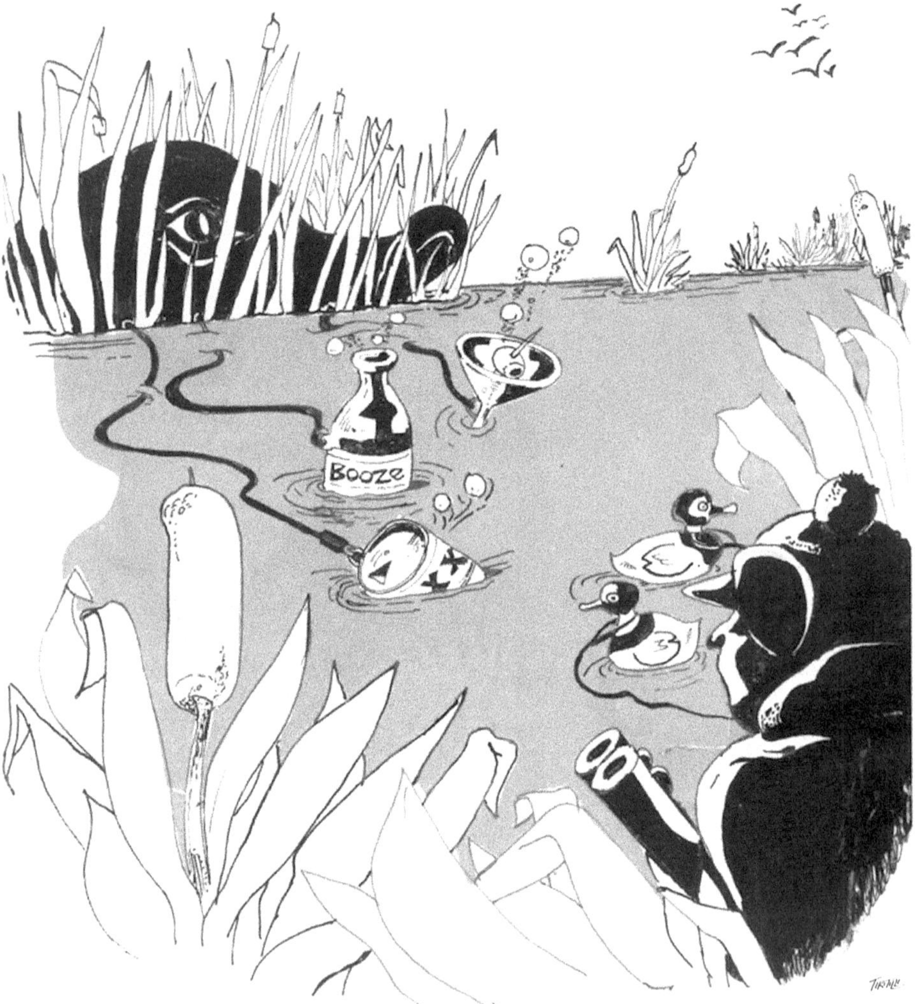
Booze

**Decoys?**

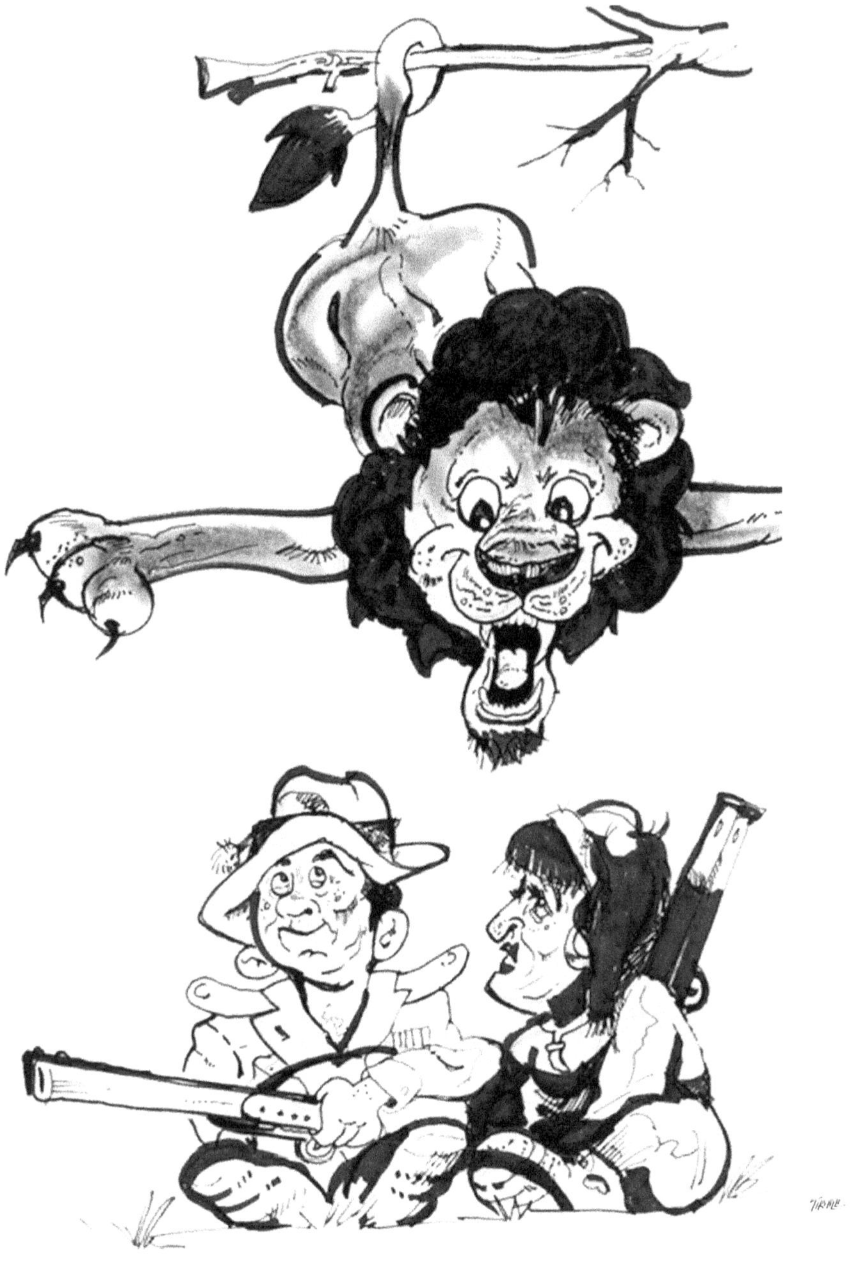

**Nature Calls**

**"Bad combination...
Buffalo roam & Antelope play!"**

www.ingramcontent.com/pod-product-compliance
Lightning Source LLC
Chambersburg PA
CBHW060555030426
42337CB00019B/3551